Deep in My Heart beats

Davena's Poetry Collection

MS. DAVENA BUCK

WORKBOOK PRESS LLC
187 E Warm Springs Rd,
Suite B285, Las Vegas, NV 89119, USA

Website: https://workbookpress.com/
Hotline: 1-888-818-4856
Email: admin@workbookpress.com

Ordering Information:
Quantity sales. Special discounts are available on quantity purchases by corporations, associations, and others. For details, contact the publisher at the address above.

ISBN-13:   978-1-953839-40-4 (Paperback Version)
                978-1-953839-42-8 (Digital Version)

REV. DATE: 12/02/2022

Deep
in
My Heartbeats:

Davena's Poetry Compilation

Written by:

Davena Buck

ACKNOWLEDGEMENT

My deepest appreciation to....

All those who encouraged me and helped me in prayer, project, and financial support to bring this book to completion.

I want to thank also my family, this book would not be complete without you.

Most importantly, my gratitude to the Lord and Savior Jesus for His grace and companionship during this project and the Holy Spirit's faithful guidance through this assignment.

INTRODUCTION

First of all, I write poetry because it is the way my mind speaks to itself. All day. Every day. Morning, noon, or night. I was never "trained" or "given a degree" in this "field." But looking back, most poets weren't either. It's a gift, a voice, a drive, a passion that just is or is not. I do not know that it can be taught or trained or molded if it is not already there. I do know I can always grow and learn. I know that some of my poems are good, some are great, and some are so-so.

I write poetry because I love it. I love reading poetry. I love thinking about poetry. I love putting my life into poetry. I love putting fairy tales into poetry, love into poetry, parenting into poetry, and social justice into poetry.

I write poetry because it helps me clarify the moment, for myself, for others, for society. I write poetry because it takes an issue or experience, wraps it in vivid feeling, and gives it to readers like a gift. I write poetry because it connects me to the world in a way nothing else ever really has. And it connects me to others in a way that nothing else ever really has. It was this thing I could do that hardly anyone else really could do. It was this thing I could do that felt real.

I write poetry because it is fun. It is much with deep level of soul joy. It is creative fun. It is like play. It is serious fun. It is like meaningful work. It is spiritual fun. It is like church and Zen and healing and prayer.

When the morning light hits your face
And you lie quietly, only your breath between us
I think about how lucky I am to know you
And I'm thankful that we have one another

live
laugh
love

Davena Buck

I want to lock you in my heart
For no one else to see
For wishes that stand forever
And stars that dance with me

For your eyes that sparkle blue
And the ripple tides you stir
When cloudy days abound
And special thoughts that were

For the long years you'll forever go
A land of great indifference Dew
For empty hours alone
Forever , Forever loving you

live
laugh
love

Davena Buck

The Pages Of My Diary

For the secret hours that steal your heart away,
for the things that whisper to you. For tucking the sweet
words out of sight, for no one else to view.

To remember the things that no one else can see.
Or those that they should never know. For keeping boxes
that are never made, for love so deep in my soul. This
is your secret box and no one else should ever see, the
flowers and the daises with in my secret love and me.

I tread not on that door, nor ever opened it with a
key. Nor stepped beyond the pages of iniquity. But I stand
by my door and there I will stay , among the flowers and
my sweet love for thee.

live
laugh
love

Davena Buck

Sometimes I wish I could be the wind traveling over the mountains to you...

Dropping gracefully, embracing your face

Sometimes I wish I were the rain tapping gently on your soul

Surrounding the mist in your heart

Sometimes I wish I were the flowers in the spring so when you touch

them I'd feel your perfume.

From time to time, I feel these urges to be everywhere you are and

though I know I cannot I want you to know my love runs as the rivers.

long and deep

and for ever flowing.

live
laugh
love

Davena Buck

Hand me the sunset
And I'll give you the stars
Wrap it in silver
Tuck it neatly in jars
Don't put it on a shelf
I ask you please
Just love me once in a lifetime
Hear my song on the breeze
Gather in the moonshine
And hold me close
Love me forever
For I love you most

live
laugh
love

Davena Buck

You say that I inspire you and I'm honored......

But what I didn't expect in all this time that I have spent with you is...

This overwhelming feeling of love that has captured my heart

I wasn't prepared to love someone and yet here you are....

And when in fact you truly are the inspiration in my life and I have discovered that I love you with all my heart.

live
laugh
love

Davena Buck

My heart melts when I see the sadness in your eyes

I want so much for you

I can't make the pain go away but I want you to know though The things of life change and that I'm always here for you... I want you to know that spring rains bring new life....

The things of flowers and the things for us to look forward too.

live
laugh
love

Davena Buck

I'm glad you make me laugh when we are together and I miss you when we are apart

And when the Island spices blow in the wind I think of how sweet our souls are as one

I'm glad you make me smile for without you I'd be lost

And though I know the direction of it ... It would not be fun

I'm glad that I love you and that you're in my life.   for counting on you has made my life more joyful

I'm glad you're there for me I'm just glad.

live
laugh
love

Davena Buck

When the morning sun peeks over the mountains and it brings forth the frost

I'm glad I awake cozy and warm snuggled next to you

Few have what we've been given... that which blooms between us at

dawn.

And throughout the day we share the little things that brings strength and love and I am so

very glad that you choose me.

live
laugh
love

Davena Buck

I noticed this morning how quiet you were
I know you have many things on your mind
I just want you to know that I love you
I'm here listening with my heart in kind.

live
laugh
love

Davena Buck

When the winter's bitter cold seeps in I choose to be in your arms ...

cozy and warm

When the spring rains pore down I choose to be by your side

When the summer sun beats down I choose to hold your hand

And when the fall leaves rattle in the wind I choose to be in your heart

I will choose you always for my love is sweeter than the melodies that

whisper in the wind.

live
laugh
love

Davena Buck

Summer's Song

When the night's sky falls obediently it brings with it, the softness of the morning dew..

The flowers smile at the mist as they reach; their petals to kiss the sun..

Songs of the birds tickle the ears as they chatter to the breeze..

I listen with my heart on these summer days as I wake next to you..

For all these things warm my soul and my pleasant love for you..

live laugh love

Davena Buck

I want you to know that when I saw you last night I knew
I would not fail to notice when your gone...

The emptiness I feel inside touches the aching in my soul

Tears flowed down my face tickling.. tearing the edges of
my heart

For the wave of passion.. the love I feel is enormous
standing on me

One day is too long to be without you... one moment in
time..

for I love you so.

live
laugh
love

Davena Buck

When I whisper your name it feels like the magic that touches the stars at night...

The twinkling in my heart explodes in fireworks of grand desire..

Painting my love ever so deeply

You are the cherished one of my heart... The star... the magic...my soul

For I have loved you always from the beginning to the end..

you are mine my love and we are one...

live
laugh
love

Davena Buck

The other evening, I took a break from life and sat among
the trees

The cool air blew brushing against my clothes calming my
personal self

My thoughts traveled across the miles over the mountains
to you

I wondered at your thoughts in this very moment in time
And if you could be thinking of me oh best friend of mine
So I'm sending you my smile along with the breeze......

And when the wind blows your way somehow ... some-
way.....

You will think of me.....

live
laugh
love

Davena Buck

When you left I thought I'd never see you again and then,

there you were and my eyes met yours...

For a moment I thought I was dreaming that you were just my wishful thinking for I had met you so many times in my mind.

And when you held me... yes held me tightly and I knew the truth

That you loved me too...

Well, I glad you came back for me for I need

you in my life

live
laugh
love

Davena Buck

I can't help but feel the tie that binds us every time we meet....

The magical connection vibrates my inner soul

It leaves me weak and I become powerless under your spell...

I am unable to grasp my thoughts clearly for, no one has ever disturbed me so, or touched me in this way...

Until you walked into my life I never knew what it was to love so deeply or to care without question

I see life more clearly and the path I want to choose, for loving you is as the rain to the rainbow and the promise that it makes.

live
laugh
love

Davena Buck

Every day I gaze at the portrait I have painted of you in my mind it's your inner soul I see.

When I enter this gallery I find heavens bliss spread before me as a table set with fine wine...

The flowers blowing gently as the winds whisper to me that your grace is one of a kind

And in this gallery the pictures set before me are of more than artistic beauty that one would normally find

For you bring more than bountiful pleasure to look upon and I'm very

glad your mine.

live
laugh
love

Davena Buck

I love the sounds that rattle from the trees as the leaves turn to red gold and brown

I love the wind that touches the eves as winter sets the stage all around I love the smell that tickles my nose as the first fall of the rain comes down

I love the snow that blankets the earth as it quiets the night to the sound But most of all I love you when all these things are around.

live
laugh
love

Davena Buck

Hello wind it's been a long, long time since I've heard from you

And today it's only in my mind

Hello friend you're in my thoughts this morning

Would you hold me one more time?

live
laugh
love

Davena Buck

Love is...

It's the sea quickening its spray against your face

The smell of fresh cut hay in a field

The warmth of hot chocolate on a cold winter's day

It's the breath of cold air that fills your lungs

The glow of the moon on the water's edge

It's the sound of crickets on a summer's night

It's holding hands, quietly walking a path

It's a feeling beyond all feeling under the sun

It's being with you.

live
laugh
love

Davena Buck

I'm waiting.... Waiting for you to come and find me...to get me to take away..

I love you...I have loved you even before I've known you, and I have known you before I've seen you

I've seen you before I've touched you...and I've touched you before I've held you

I've held you before I've love you and I love you before the rain, the wind, the moon and stars.

I feel you close... I hear your heart beat and if I listen in the quiet hours I feel your breath on my face your touch...

I know your lips... your caress, and I drink in the blue of your eyes... I know you and I wait... I wait for you

In this peaceful quiet time, I wait for you to come and you will..

I know this, you will....

live
laugh
love

Davena Buck

God's hand is in the music that's gentle in the night

Flowing on the breezes like the waves of radiant light

His hands are the ones that mold to be gentle and to be kind

To breath the air of love for you is only his to find

live laugh love

Davena Buck

To share with you...

Today I smelled the trees and it took me back a ways

When I was just a child and things were pleasant in those days

Of times that joy of life was ever so simple

And the breeze always blew and the night lay ever so gentle It took me by surprise to remember this so well

My days of yonder years and the many things that I could smell.

live
laugh
love

Davena Buck

I've never danced in the moonlight or whispered in the rain

I've never felt the romance that some say brings spring

I've never known the gentle touches of the hair brushed from my face

I've never saw the longing as in the morning we embraced

I've never known the song we danced to as the music's sweet melody

Or the laughter rising from me as I played before I cried

I never knew your arms around me as you whispered I love you

Until today that is...............I never knew, I just never knew.

live laugh love

Davena Buck

You have worked very hard this year and sooo..

I wish for you all the pleasant things in life

Rainbows, Moonbeams and stars

You deserve the best of the spring rains

Walks on a moonlit night and no sorrows in sight

A good book, curled up by a fire and all the friends you desire........

May you find what you need in life....

live
laugh
love

Davena Buck

I'm sorry

I'm sorry I made you cry, it wasn't my intention when I spoke those

words to you today

I forget about your gentle side when I want only my way and

because it seems so important to me I hurt you in ways I do not intend.

I'm sorry

If I could wish upon a star Id wish for it to take the words back and to never say those things to you again

The things I said were not kind and I ask that you forgive me....

Most of all I love you.   ...and I'm sorry.

live
laugh
love

Davena Buck

Sometimes I forget to watch the sunset with you.......

Sometimes I forget to tell you that I watch you while you sleep

And sometimes I forget to say I love you and more

But every day when I look at you I remember, I remember what forever

Is for..

live
laugh
love

Davena Buck

Have I told you

How well your hand fits mine and when the wind blows it seems to stop all passage of time.

How the earth stood still when you looked into my eyes and the stars burned brighter when day turned to night

Have I told you

How the light shines within you when you brush the hair from my face

or how the love I feel for you my heart quickens a pace

Have I told you

That you are like no other that I have ever known but without you I

would be so alone

live
laugh
love

Davena Buck

Tucked down inside my heart is my love for you...

Sewn into the edges are pieces of the words you have spoken to me.

The night is mine when the lights go out in my eyes and dreams take me to places with you I've never been.

I've danced the evening in your arms and sailed the seas, walked the rain forest and shared a picnic among the trees.

We've shared snowball fights, laughter and held hands while sitting quietly listening to the crackling fire.

You've brushed the hair from my face and touched me tenderly as you pulled me close; your strong arms around me.. yes these are the things I feel for you but most of all, let me love you.

live
laugh
love

Davena Buck

The sun goes down and the tide goes out
Let it take all your heartaches and troubles....
Let them drift away with each lap of the wave
And wake in the morning to a new dawn...

live
laugh
love

Davena Buck

I want you to know that when I saw you last night I knew
I would not fail to notice when your gone....

The emptiness I feel inside touches the aching in my soul

Tears flowed down my face trickling...tearing the edges of
my heart

For the wave of passion...   the love I feel is enormous
standing on me

One day is too long to be without you ....one moment in
time...

for I love you so..

live
laugh
love

Davena Buck

I remember the night you proposed to me

How warm I felt inside

The words you spoke as you held my hand and the stars
that shined in your eyes

I'm thankful that you choose me that night when we
heard the music play

And God gave me you.....my one true love on our wedding
day

live
laugh
love

Davena Buck

I thought of you this morning when I opened my eyes

It brought warmth to my heart as I began this day

Reminding me of our special friendship that only we share

I wanted to tell you that I love you and how much you mean to me

And if ever you need me that I am here

live
laugh
love

Davena Buck

...THE END...

www.ingramcontent.com/pod-product-compliance
Lightning Source LLC
Chambersburg PA
CBHW051601120626
46551CB00013B/1614